D1716085

Division Gymnastics

Book Seven of
The Gift of Numbers
Math Fantasy Curriculum

$45 \div 5 = 9$

$28 \div 4 = 7$

Rachel Rogers and Joe Lineberry

Illustrations by ARTE RAVE

$64 \div 8 = 8$

To Lydia and Anna,
Yay! The mystery of the
disappearing numbers
is solved!
Joe Lineberry
3/14/2022

PROSPECTIVE PRESS
ACADEMICS

an imprint of

PROSPECTIVE PRESS LLC

1959 Peace Haven Rd, #246, Winston-Salem, NC 27106 U.S.A.
www.prospectivepress.com

Published in the United States of America by PROSPECTIVE PRESS LLC

DIVISION GYMNASTICS

Text copyright © Rachel Rogers and Joe Lineberry, 2022
All rights reserved.
The authors' moral rights have been asserted.

Illustrations by ARTE RAVE
© Prospective Press, 2022
All rights reserved.
The illustrator's moral rights have been asserted.

ISBN 978-1-943419-13-5

ProP-H001

Division Gymnastics is the seventh volume in the Gift of Numbers math fantasy curriculum. For information on additional volumes in the series or for bulk sales, please send inquiries to education@prospectivepress.com

Printed in the United States of America
First hardcover printing, February, 2022

The text of this book is typeset in Mouse Memoirs
Accent text is typeset in Galindo

Dedicated to our proficient publisher

Coach Winner and Coach Success were hurrying toward the front door of More Hospital. They were obviously excited. King Less and Detective Science were hurrying out the same door of the hospital.

THUMP! THUD!

The two groups crashed into each other. They were all dazed, lying on the ground.

King Less was the first one to speak. "What's the rush?"

"You won't believe this," said Coach Winner, now sitting up. "I received an email from Dream Princess. She is challenging us to a gymnastics competition next week."

"Small numbers are usually better gymnasts," added Coach Success. "We need athletic small numbers, and we need them fast."

"The doctors helped us before," continued Coach Success. "They made big numbers for us using multiplication. Our best athletes are now big football players. We need the doctors to make them small again."

Doctor Even had rushed to an upstairs window when he heard the crash. He overheard the coaches talking. He began thinking about how to create small numbers quickly.

Detective Science started talking. "This is funny," said the detective. "You got an invitation to take your team to Dream Princess. We don't have an invitation, but we are running to see the princess now."

"Why do you want to see Dream Princess?" asked Coach Winner.

"Her company bottles mountain water," replied the king. "And our experiment showed her mountain water is causing our numbers to disappear."

"Wow! That is big news! But can you wait a few days? You can go to see her as part of our team," said Coach Winner. "You might learn more that way."

"I agree. Please come with us, King Less," added Coach Success. "You've met Dream Princess. I heard that she is a ghostly zero. Who knows what she will do?"

Doctor Even surprised everyone by shouting from the window.

He shouted down to the coaches, "Bring in your big number football players. Doctor Odd and I will make some athletic small numbers for you. We may need to create a new math operation!"

The detective ran back toward the hospital door, shouting, "I want to help, too."

"Doctor Even and Detective Science found Doctor Odd relaxing in his office. "No time to spare," exclaimed Doctor Even. He quickly described the coaches' need for small numbers for the gymnastic team.

"You used multiplication to make big numbers quickly for the football teams," said Detective Science. "You need to create the **inverse** operation to multiplication."

"**W**hoa!" said Doctor Odd. "Big word. What do you mean saying we need to create an 'inverse' operation?"

The detective explained, "Think about it. Subtraction is the **opposite** operation for addition. You use subtraction to undo an addition problem."

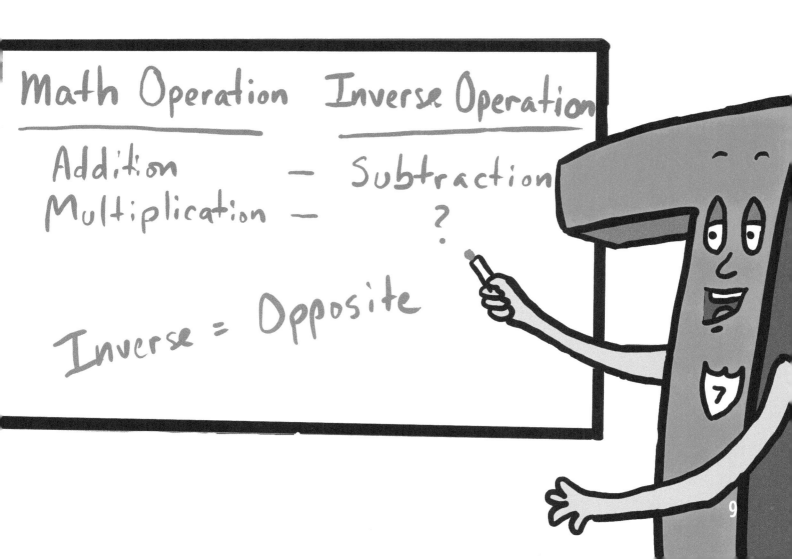

Math Operation   Inverse Operation

Addition   —   Subtraction
Multiplication   —   ?

Inverse = Opposite

"Detective Science continued, "You can add 7 + 8 = 15

Then you use subtraction to undo it:

$$15 - 8 = 7$$

So subtraction is the inverse of addition. It undoes the addition operation.

To make small numbers now, you need to undo the football player multiplication operations."

Doctor Even confidently turned to Doctor Odd.
"We can do this. I'll meet you at the lab."

You guessed it. After a few hours in the lab, the doctors discovered the opposite operation of multiplication. They discovered **division**. Division became the newest member of the operation club.

OPERATION CLUB

OPERATION	ANSWER
ADDITION	⟶ SUM
SUBTRACTION	⟶ DIFFERENCE
MULTIPLICATION	⟶ PRODUCT
DIVISION	⟶ QUOTIENT

The large number football players lined up outside the operation rooms to try the new division operation.

$$64 \div 8 = 8$$

$$\text{Then } 8 \div 4 = 2$$

In two quick steps of division, Doctor Even reduced a big 64 to a small, athletic 2.

Doctor Odd was also able to make small numbers fast with division.

$$81 \div 9 = 9$$

$$\text{Then } 9 \div 3 = 3$$

When the doctor finished this operation, he had a new idea. He caught up with Doctor Even in the hall outside his operation room.

"Hey, Doctor Even," shouted Doctor Odd. "We can make small numbers even faster. Remember the multiplication rule of 1? You know, when you multiply 1 times any number you get that number. Like, 99 x 1 = 99."

"Yes," said Doctor Even. "Now that you say it, I do remember that math fact."

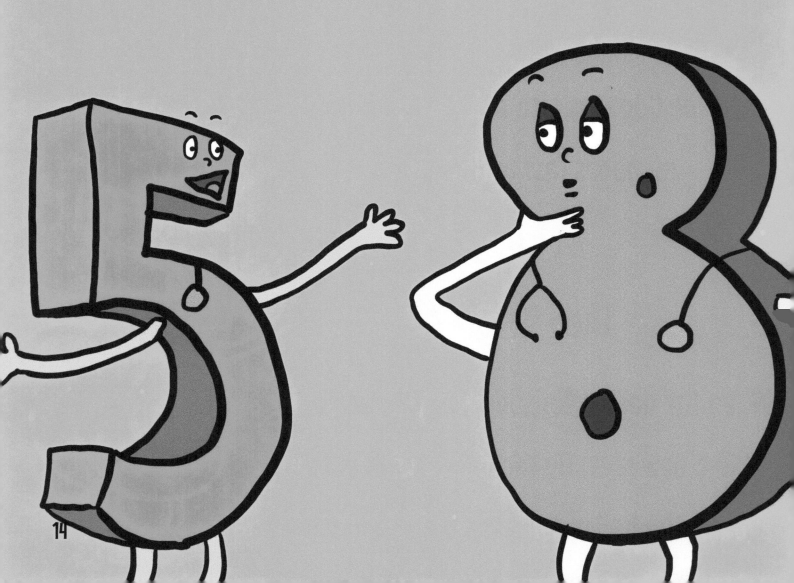

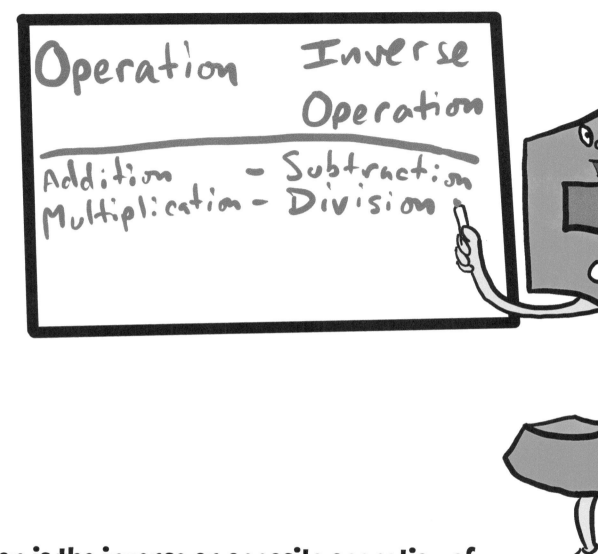

"**Division** is the inverse or opposite operation of multiplication," said Doctor Odd. "So we can undo that operation with division and get a small 1 quickly. Watch:

$$99 \div 99 = 1$$

We can divide any number by itself and get a 1 with one step."

"Here is another idea," said Doctor Even. "Remember how any even number can be divided into two equal groups with no leftover. For example:

80 is made up of two equal groups of 40. That is the same as

$$80 = 2 \times 40.$$

1	2	3	4	5	6	7	8	9	10
11	12	13	14	15	16	17	18	19	20
21	22	23	24	25	26	27	28	29	30
31	32	33	34	35	36	37	38	39	40

41	42	43	44	45	46	47	48	49	50
51	52	53	54	55	56	57	58	59	60
61	62	63	64	65	66	67	68	69	70
71	72	73	74	75	76	77	78	79	80

If we undo that multiplication operation with division, we can quickly make a 2."

$$80 \div 40 = 2$$

Using division, the doctors created an athletic team of small numbers in one day. The two coaches trained their new gymnastics team every day. They wanted them to be at their best when they went to compete with Dream Princess's team.

The big day arrived for the gymnastics event. King Less and Detective Science went with the gymnastics team to meet Dream Princess.

"Dream Princess was excited to see King Less again. She also was glad to finally meet the famous Detective Science. She invited both of them to sit with her at the gymnastics arena.

When the king and the detective arrived at the arena, the two gymnastic teams were warming up. But the princess was late getting to her seat.

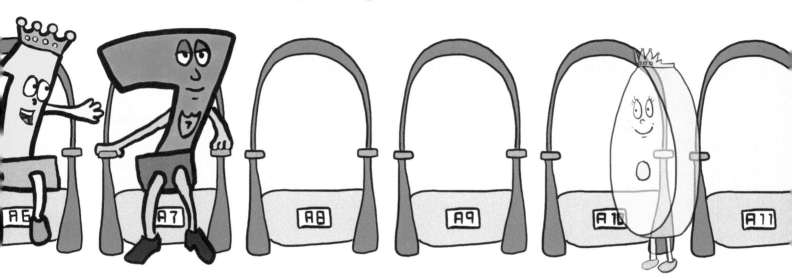

"Where have you been?" King Less asked Dream Princess as she arrived. "Is everything okay?"

"Sure," replied the princess. "Some of our Magic Formula #199 had gone bad. It doesn't work well after two days. I was throwing the leftover potion into the river."

"Remind me," said the King. "What is Magic Formula #199?"

"Don't you remember?" responded Dream Princess. "You didn't want to buy this one. This is the formula that helps numbers disappear."

"And you throw your leftover potion in the river?" asked Detective Science. "We need to talk to you about—"

The detective couldn't finish his sentence.

Suddenly, number 4 appeared in the empty seat beside the detective. Number 4 wasn't there two seconds ago. But now he was sitting there, yawning.

At first, Detective Science was so shocked that he couldn't speak. Then he stammered, "W-wh-what is going on?"

Dream Princess leaned over to talk to number 4. "Why don't you tell them where you have been?"

"Let me catch my breath," replied number 4. He took a deep breath and began his story, "I took some formula #199 yesterday and disappeared."

"You're wacky," interrupted King Less.
"Why would you do that?"

"Let me finish," said number 4. "I disappeared here, but I appeared in the world of people. I was sent to Shane's kitchen. His dad was making lunch bags for Shane and his three sisters."

"Then what happened?" asked Detective Science. The detective was no longer shocked. Now he felt excited and curious. He was hearing more clues about the mystery of the missing numbers.

"I was floating in the air near the ceiling," explained number 4. "A lot of other numbers were floating there, too. No people could see us.

"Shane's dad asked Shane to calculate how many grapes he and his sisters could have for lunch. Dad wanted each of them to have the same number of grapes."

Number 4 continued, "Shane counted the grapes in two clusters. One cluster had 13 grapes and the other cluster had 15 grapes. So Shane starting writing on his paper:

$$13 + 15 = \square$$

As he was writing, I watched a 13 and a 15 drop out of the air onto Shane's paper."

The detective interrupted, "I am guessing that when Shane was writing the answer, a 28 appeared out of the air. It fell into the box on Shane's paper."

"How did you know?" asked number 4. "Have you been to the world of people, too?"

"Actually no," said the detective. "But I would like to go there."

"So, number 4, you were floating with other numbers" asked King Less. "When did you get involved?"

Number 4 smiled. "I came down on the next step," he said. "Shane divided the 28 grapes by 4 children, so I dropped onto his paper as he was writing the **divisor**."

28 grapes ÷ 4 children = ☐

"When he solved the problem," continued number 4, "a 7 emerged from the air and fell in the box on his paper. It was the answer to the problem, called the **quotient**. His dad needed to put 7 grapes into each of their 4 lunch bags."

13 grapes + 15 grapes =
28 grapes

28 grapes ÷ 4 children =
7 grapes per child

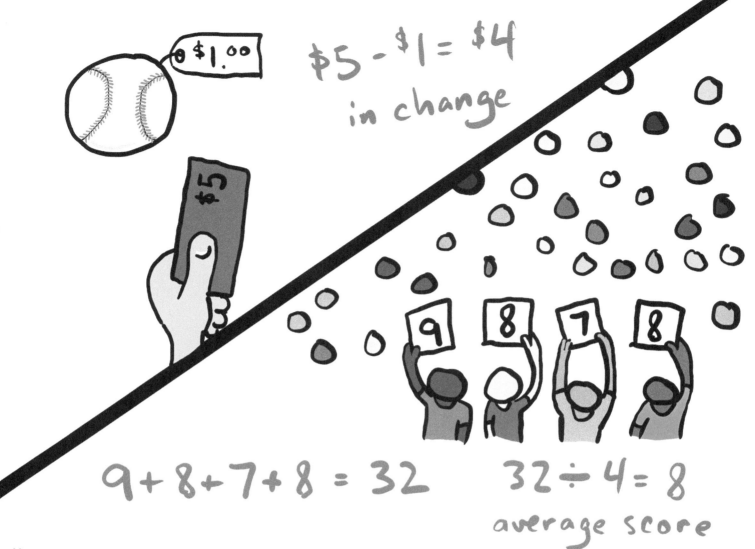

$5 - $1 = $4
in change

9 + 8 + 7 + 8 = 32   32 ÷ 4 = 8
average score

"I was in more math operations during the next few days," said number 4. "Then I got tired. I yawned, and poof! I came back and landed in this seat beside you."

"That is amazing," exclaimed King Less. "We have been trying to keep numbers from disappearing so future boys and girls would have enough numbers."

"Now we discover that numbers disappear so they can go help the world of people," added Detective Science.

Dream Princess turned to King Less. "That's what I tried to tell you earlier," said the princess. "We disappear to give children numbers for their math operations. It's our gift of numbers to boys and girls."

"Well, I changed my mind," responded the king. "Now I want to buy formula #199. Then our numbers can go help girls and boys solve their math problems.

"And we really won't run out of numbers. Our numbers can just yawn and come back to our world."

"Yay!" exclaimed Detective Science. "Look at all we did to solve the mystery of the missing numbers."

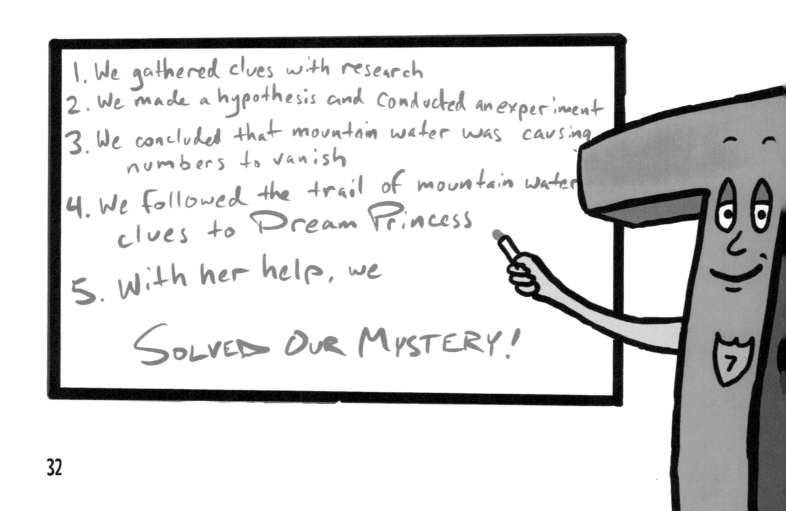

1. We gathered clues with research
2. We made a hypothesis and conducted an experiment
3. We concluded that mountain water was causing numbers to vanish
4. We followed the trail of mountain water clues to Dream Princess
5. With her help, we

SOLVED OUR MYSTERY!

The detective then turned to Dream Princess. He spoke kindly but firmly, "Thanks so much for helping us solve our mystery. But we need to talk about you dumping old formula #199 into the river . . ."

The End

Division Gymnastics Exercises

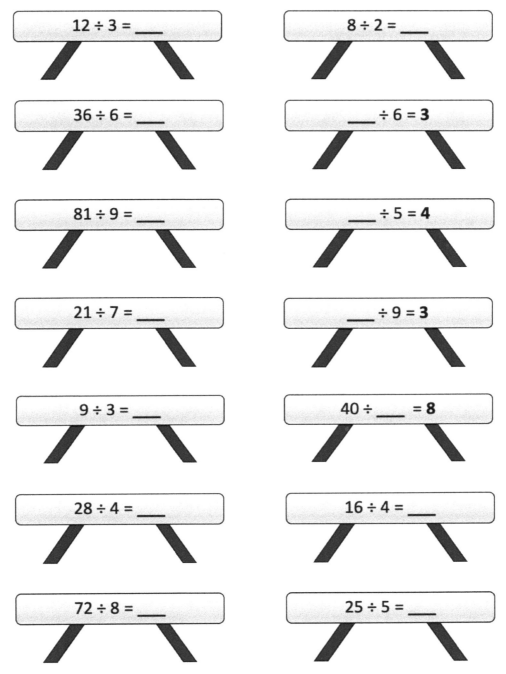

$12 \div 3 = \underline{\quad}$

$8 \div 2 = \underline{\quad}$

$36 \div 6 = \underline{\quad}$

$\underline{\quad} \div 6 = 3$

$81 \div 9 = \underline{\quad}$

$\underline{\quad} \div 5 = 4$

$21 \div 7 = \underline{\quad}$

$\underline{\quad} \div 9 = 3$

$9 \div 3 = \underline{\quad}$

$40 \div \underline{\quad} = 8$

$28 \div 4 = \underline{\quad}$

$16 \div 4 = \underline{\quad}$

$72 \div 8 = \underline{\quad}$

$25 \div 5 = \underline{\quad}$

1. In the world of people, Diego has made presents for his family. He now wants to put a nice bow of ribbon on each present. He has 15 feet of ribbon, and each gift needs 3 feet of ribbon. How many gifts can Diego wrap using this ribbon? Show your work.

2. Diego's friend Sara is playing the role of a princess in the school play. Sara can practice saying her lines in 10 minutes. If she wants to practice saying her lines 12 times before the play, how many hours does she need to practice? Show your work.

Division Gymnastics Exercise Solutions

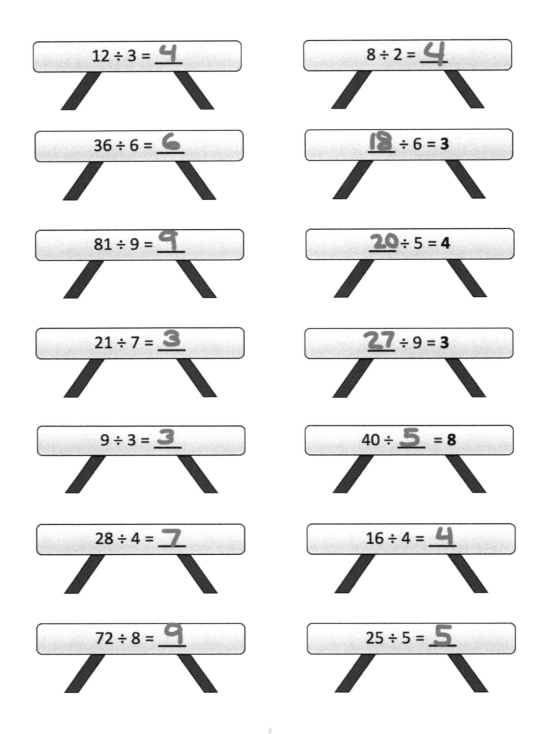

12 ÷ 3 = 4

8 ÷ 2 = 4

36 ÷ 6 = 6

18 ÷ 6 = 3

81 ÷ 9 = 9

20 ÷ 5 = 4

21 ÷ 7 = 3

27 ÷ 9 = 3

9 ÷ 3 = 3

40 ÷ 5 = 8

28 ÷ 4 = 7

16 ÷ 4 = 4

72 ÷ 8 = 9

25 ÷ 5 = 5

1. 15 feet ÷ 3 feet per gift = 5 gifts

2. 10 minutes per practice session x 12 practice sessions = 120 minutes
   120 minutes ÷ 60 minutes per hour = 2 hours

Discussion Questions

1. How would you end this story?

   - What did Detective Science say after he said, "But we need to talk about you dumping old formula #199 into the river"?

   - How did Dream Princess respond?

   - Then what happened?

2. Look up at the ceiling. How many numbers do you think are invisibly floating above you?

3. Why did numbers who lived in Dream Princess's region want to disappear?

4. Division is the _____ operation of multiplication. What does this mean?

5. How did Shane use division to help his dad with the grapes? What other math operation did he use?

6. What surprised you about the story in *Division Gymnastics*?

About the Authors

Rachel Rogers
retired from Old Richmond Elementary School, Winston-Salem, NC, after more than 42 years of teaching first, second, and third graders.

Joe Lineberry
told similar stories to his sons when they were growing up. He is also the author of *Let's Stop Playing Games: Finding Freedom in Authentic Living.*

About the Books

The Gift of Numbers
is a math fantasy curriculum that combines literature and mathmatics in a fun, age-appropriate series for second- and third-grade students.

Volume 1: *Saved by Addition*

Volume 2: *Surprised by Subtraction*

Volume 3: *Graphing the Mystery*

Volume 4: *Adventure with Fractions*

Volume 5: *Multiplication Football*

Volume 6: *The Experiment Game*

Volume 7: *Division Gymnastics*

CPSIA information can be obtained
at www.ICGtesting.com
Printed in the USA
BVHW021420180222
629401BV00001B/7